# Heart Poet

A collection of poems from my heart to yours

## Fatima Sham

BookLeaf Publishing

India | USA | UK

Presentation by *BookLeaf Publishing*

Web: www.bookleafpub.com

E-mail: info@bookleafpub.com

ISBN: 9789360945343

First edition 2024

For: Mama, Baby and Mikhail..


I am because you are

# ACKNOWLEDGEMENT

There are so many people to thank and a multitude of gratitude. There have been many sources of inspiration and support. I have been so blessed to be able to have found deep connections and truly found my tribe.

My mom and dad - who, throughout my childhood have taught me love and equality from the inside out. Love you guys. My sister who is my everything. My husband Nabil who has supported all my good and bad ideas. My son Mikhail who is an old soul and brings me so much love, joy and pride.

And in no particular order I wanted to thank:

My mother-in-law Ruhiya and sister-in-law Lubeina. My nephew Qasim who is such a considerate and caring soul. My Nani, Nana, Dadi and late Pappaji who have been pillars of strength. Lots of love to my brothers-in-law Akil and Mustafa and my two nieces whom I adore - Sophia and Samara.

Francoise - who helps me get my head from the clouds and puts my feet firmly on the ground. Tarmo - my steady diplomatic sounding board, Caroline - a source of endless humor and joy. Namrata, Zahabiya, Malika and Siddhi - my school friends whom I've grown up with, for understanding me and being my safe space to express myself. Shruti, Sonal, Marzia - my childhood friends whom I can vent to. Prianca - who I can get real with. Gayatri - who taught me gratitude and kindness. Raksha - my shining light of perspectives.

My sisters - Jumana and Nishreen - who have seen me through the dark and the light. Alefia, Insiya, Zoya, Zahra Rashida and Farida - strong, courageous and just inspiring. Alefiya and her daughter Sofiya -whose friendship I am so grateful for.

My brothers - Abedin, Qadir, Hozefa, Ali, Juzer, Huzefa, Khaled, Rajiv.

My mommy's friends who have seen me at my worst and still decided to stick by me - Bhakti, Neha, Anuja, Aarti, Neelanjana, Rachael, Sonali, Pallavi, Aashmi. Some connections are just from the heart - Tasneem, Sakina, Murtaza, Jyoti, Vihal, Anuj, Kanchan, Aditya (Parikh), Sebastian and Firdaus.

People who are always there to support me and celebrate my wins - Ash, Anosh, Surabhi, Aditya, Deaon, Kunal, Rishita, Ashish and Jinal.

My support staff - Nirali, Yasmin and Anwar who take care of me and my house in the most kind and caring of ways.

This would have not come about without the help of BookLeaf Publishers who encourage so many budding writers to follow their dreams. Ivy, Mujtaba and Jaya who have worked on the book with me, I am ever so grateful.

Special thanks to - Abhilasha who helped me bring my heart_poet_ Instagram to life and for being such a support in my life.

Lastly I want to thank and send deep gratitude to all the ones that hurt me, all the things that I thought were for me but weren't, all the pain and the heartbreak without which the poetry would have never been possible.

# PREFACE

Thank you for buying this book. It was really scary writing down all that was inside me. Leaving myself exposed and vulnerable. What would people think of my heartache and my pain, my silly fleeting thoughts or observations or of me? The one thought that made me do it, was that even if one person can relate, or smile or feel less alone - I would do it. And thus began the Instagram page heart_poet_ and now this book. I have loved every minute of it. The poems are meant to be read in no particular order - straight from my heart to yours. Happy reading!

# FOREWORD

Fatima has a relatable poetry writing style that allows you to look deeper at everyday thoughts. Her accessible writing makes you think about seemingly simple things like time, love, relationships and heartbreak, all with just a few lines. I've always known her to be a creative energy, whether it was with her words, art or being a genius in the kitchen. Her ability to introspect and add a fresh perspective to everything makes it a pleasure to read her poetry. We are all so proud of her, and everything she has achieved and will continue to achieve

Sarah Sham,
Principle designer,
Essajees Ateliere

# (H) ART

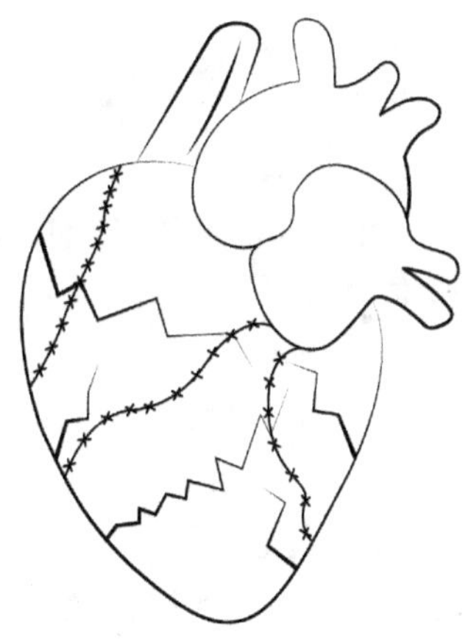

I ripped my beating heart
Right out of my chest
Crushed it into a paste
And used the pulverized bits
To paint my life red

# NOSTALGIA

It went down so smooth
The spicy potatoes,
Flaky golden pastry
and a crunchy crust
I took in the aromas
Of this deep fried deliciousness
Taking me back
To my childhood
To the school canteen
To my friend's homes
To the theatres of old
Two samosas, shared together
More than sustenance
A comfort, an emotion a memory

# TRADITIONS

Same time of the year
Same people
Same familiarity
Real conversations
Laughter and love
Some traditions are meant to last forever

# ADDICT

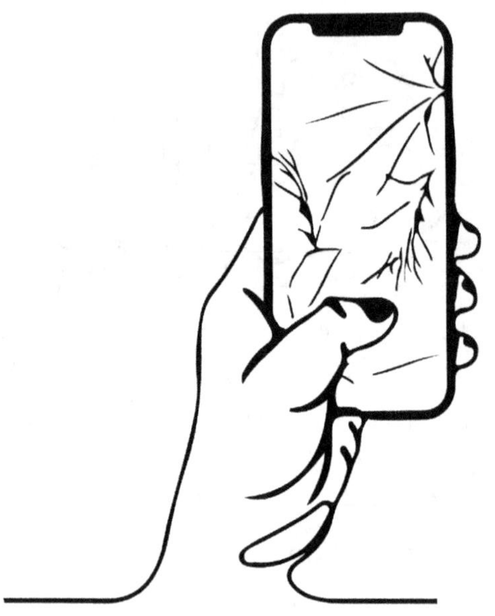

I took a breath to look up
Birds
Trees
Concrete jungle
Wires entangled
Clouds
Sky
Before my eyes go back to my phone

# WHAT IS POETRY?

To change one's perspectives
To bring out a memory
To touch someone's soul
To strike a chord deep inside
With nothing but
the delicate arrangement
of selected words, strung together
THAT is Poetry

# ME VS MYSELF

Re-running arguments
In my head
That I should have won
Long after they are done

# ABANDONED

When we refuse
to abandon others
Despite extenuating circumstances
We choose
To abandon
Ourselves

# THE WORST ANIMAL

The value of human lives
has been reduced to
the amount of money they have
Imagine the fate of the animals

# TO MY LOVED ONES

I don't have
All the answers
I can't solve
Your problems
It is not possible
To take
The pain away
All I can do
Is be there for you
Sit with you
Through the storm
Listen to you
Crack silky jokes sometimes
Till we come out
On the other side
Side by side
Together

# PATRIARCHY

Men have made
religion, laws and rules
Suited to their
perspectives and prerogatives
Women,
it's time to
Stand up and question

# IF YOU FEEL IT SAY IT

Why must it be this way?
Why can't we just say
I love you, anytime any day
If we say it too much, we're desperate
If we say it too little we are cold
If we say to a lover first
It becomes a power play
If it is not immediately said back
It is misconstrued
Father's don't say it enough
But then it is valued more
Mother's say it all the time
But then it isn't valued at all
Why Why Why
Why must it be this way?
Why can't we just say
I love you, anytime any day

# THE NOW

We live in the regrets of the past
We live in the stress of the future
When do we live at all?

# DON'T GIVE IT UP (?)

If magic happens
When you don't give up,
When do you wait until?
Are you hanging on to a foolish hope,
Or is your luck about to change?
Is it keeping you in the past,
Or keeping you going for the future?
Should you stay invested,
Or cash out and choose a new path?
Do we define time in years,
Or with resources and emotions?
Is it that the miracles happen
Only once you've hit rock bottom?
We may never know

# UNREQUITED LOVE

I gave my heart to you
And all you did
Was walk away
How cruel was that?
But then you turned and looked at me
and said, "Meow"
and my whole world turned around
and I gave my heart to you again

# TABLE

Oh honey,
You don't have to
Bring something to the table
you ARE the table

# UN CLENCH

The Bed
The Pot
The relief
The comfort.
I'm home

# MAGICAL

Let there be
Magic sprinkled like fairy dust
All along the way
So the way
Is as magical
As the destination

# (N)EVER LOVE

The first
The last
The only
Why not start with yourself?

# BITTER

The bitterness
I have been feeling
Is like Venom
Entering unwillingly into my bloodstream
and poisoning my soul

# THE AWARD

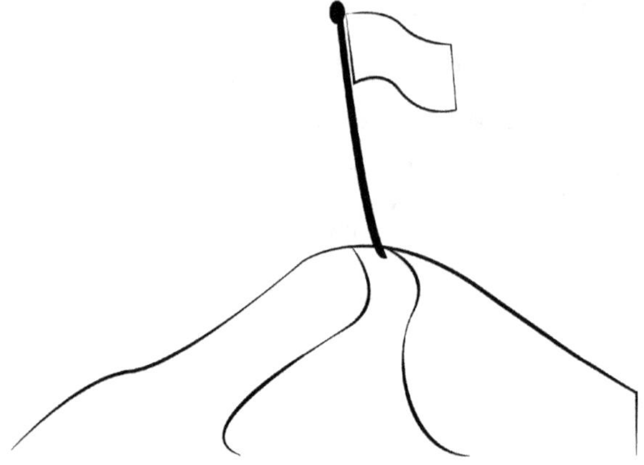

In the end,
who is coming
to give me an award
for all the things I sacrificed and gave up
to please others?

# KINDNESS

People who touch your soul
Will always remain
Somewhere inside you
As part of your world
It could be a small act
A glance and a smile
A conversation
A laugh, or
Sharing of a mint
But the memories have
An everlasting imprint
Of the kindness you shared

# SALAD

My heart feels
Bitter
like kale
Sour
like grapefruit
And burnt
like charcoal
A deliciously poignant salad of emotions

# FINISH LINE

Rest
But don't stop
Go slowly
The road may be
Winding,
Uphill,
fraught with stones;
Rest
But don't stop
Take small steps
Catch your breath,
Rest
But don't stop
So that
When the time comes
You can sprint
Full speed
Without obstacles
Towards the finish line

# YOUNIQUE

We are all one
Yet
We are one in a billion

# UNFILTERED

When
I can be free
To be
Completely
Unfiltered me,
Is when
I know
I love you

# HIDE AND SEEK

The joy you seek
is not to be chased
but to be experienced;
Here
Now and
In this moment

# HEART EYE EMOJI

When you love someone
Their face looks like
The most beautiful in the world
Their eyes look like
A galaxy of stars
Their scars, pimples and blemishes
Fade away into a blur
If only Instagram had a filter like this

# HOPE

Hope means that
The wonders of this world
Are yet to be experienced
The best of times
yet to come
bit by bit
day by day
Hope is the journey

# DEFINING

Height, weight, skin colour
Can never define;
Honey
You are divine
It is your personality
That will always
Truly outshine

# MAMA

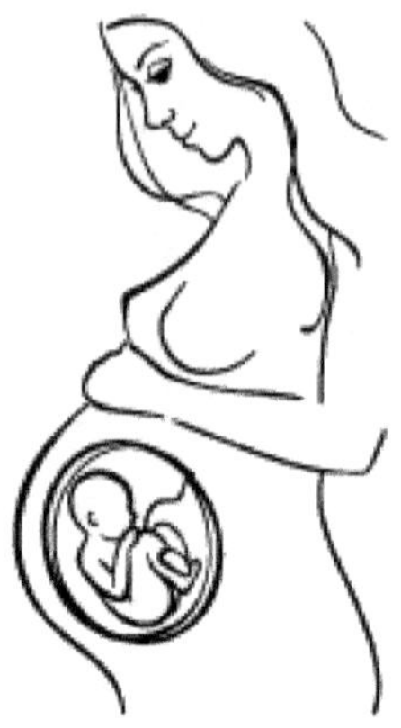

What is forever?
A fleeting moment
that captures eternity
When you smiled at me

# OPPORTUNITIES

Things not working out
In a manner you thought
Left you with a hole
Filled with darkness
Leaving you space
To fill to the brim
All the things
That bring you light

# WORTHY?

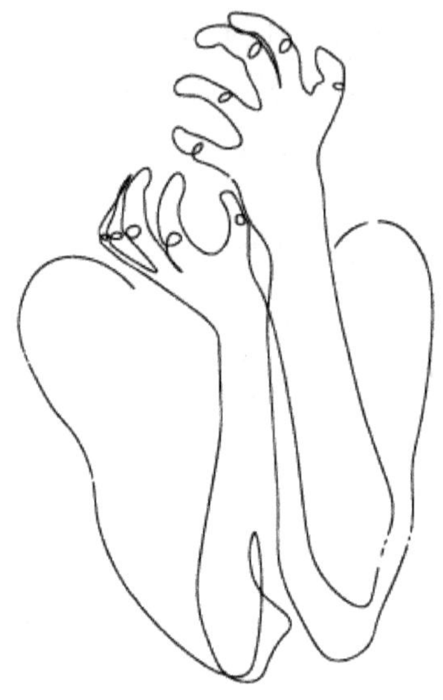

Hello insecurity
my old friend
Rearing your ugly head again

# THE ACHIEVER

Achieving anything,
Worthy and fulfilling
Takes blood, sweat and tears
Forgoing your fears
Resilience
Sacrifice
Nothing but your best effort
Will suffice
The grind and consistency
Will be rewarded eventually
When you achieve anything
Worthy and fulfilling

# IT STARTS WITH US

If you
Don't believe
in yourself
Who will?

# LIFE IN PLASTIC

Fantastic
Filters
Fillers
Flamboyant
Fabulous
Fake

# THE DEEP DARK SPACES

Be positive
Be grateful
but what happens to the ones
in the deep dark spaces
in the cracks and crevices
What happens in the shadows
when the monsters raise their ugly heads
What happens when
you question every word
you ever said
every choice you ever made
and wish you chose better?
What happens after the day
that you knowingly made
the worst decisions;
You veered off course
you fucked things up
you lost your mind
you lost your heart...
How do you bring back those times
how do you stay sane
how do you grow
To be grateful again?

# TUNNEL OF LIGHT

Go into
The sadness
The discomfort
The heartbreak
Through to the other side

# MONSOON FOREST

The wind howled with delight
Passing a joke on through the night
The leaves shook gleefully
The grass below swayed merrily
The sky joined them in the downpour
Thunder with laughter roared
Raindrops fell thick and fast
Monsoon was here at last

# SHACKLES

Are we really free
Or chained to our phones?

# JUST BREATHE

Just breathe
It is that simple my love
Slow deep breaths
One after the other
Everything may be falling apart
There is a gaping hole in your heart
You may not be able to see
The long term view right now
Just breathe
Slow deep breaths
One after the other
We will find
The calm strength and courage
One breath at a time

# SCARS

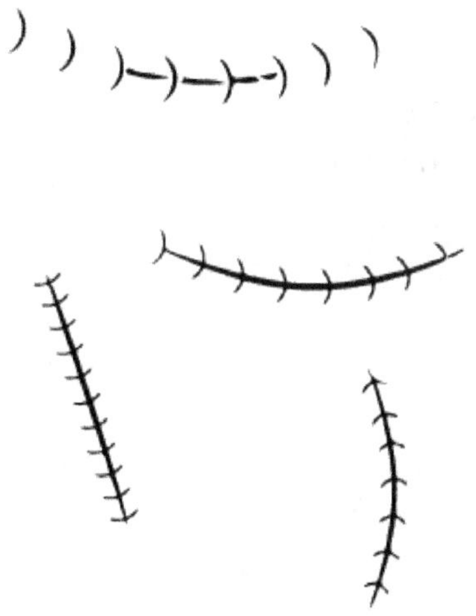

We are never prepared
For the time
Our loved ones
leave us
It slices right through the heart
Oozing blood
Leaving a deep wound
And even over time
Although the cut heals,
The scars will always remain

# DREAMER

Some days
I dream
And
Some days
ARE the dream

# THE "UGLY" SECRET

The wrinkles around my eyes
tell me I have laughed out loud
The dark spots and pigmentation
tell me I have danced in the sun and sea
My stretch marks show me
how many meals I've had
surrounded by loved ones
eating and drinking too much
yet
I feel the need to hide, correct or reverse it
as if it was something ugly

# MIND GYMNASTICS

My mind runs
A million miles a minute
Looping and swaying
Jumping to all conclusions
Somersaulting and twisting
Like a graceful gymnast.
Only difference is
I have to practise
for it to stop

# EVERYTHING & NOTHING

Love has
No description,
No definition;
But yet
It encompasses everything
and defines all

# CARPE DIEM

Wake up
Shake up
Your body, inhibitions and lethargy
And
Seize the day

# LETTING THEM IN

The ones closest to us,
Our people
Wield an extraordinary power;
To lift us up
Or put us down

# OVER IT

The over pleasing
The over explaining
The over thinking
I'm over it

# TIK TOK

The universe has perfect timing
that we can only see
in hindsight

# PLUG AND PLAY

Sometimes I wish
That I was a switch
So my feelings
Could be
Turned on and off
On demand

# ADULTING

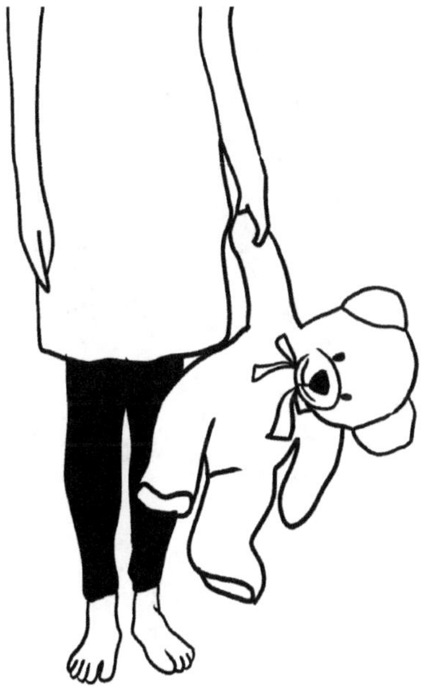

How do we decide
between pursuing what's meant for you
and letting go of what's not?

# TALK TO ME

Words hurt
But
What hurts more
Is words unspoken

# GO GIRL

New day
Same me
Same consistency
Same persistency
So I can be
The same but better me

# INFECTION

Energy is infectious
It is invisible
Sometimes inexplicable
You can catch it from anyone
Anyone can catch it from you,
So share your enthusiasm
And spread the laughter
And be the new energy pandemic

# WORDS

Make
Shape
Create
Our reality
What words will you tell yourself today?

# HELP

Helping others
Helps me
Get over myself

# SHOULDER

Some friends are like shoulders
steady, stable, strong
something you can rely on
something you can cry on

# ALONE

My every struggle
has been fought before
My every problem
has been solved already
Then why do I feel so alone?

# TEAR

It is no coincidence
That tear drops
Share the same spelling
As tear
Tears fall
When we are torn apart
Tearing at the seams

# CONFUSED

We must not chase joy
yet
We must seek it

# HEAD OVER HEART

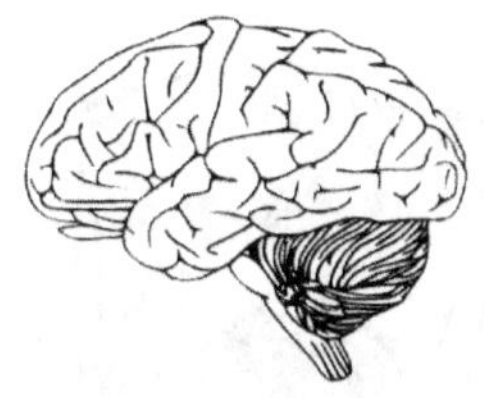

My head knows the answers
The sensible rational solutions
If only my heart would listen

# NOT TODAY

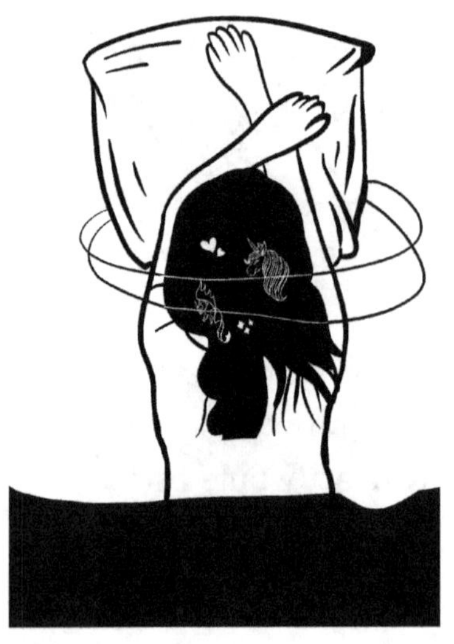

12 year olds are out there
Starting businesses
Conquering the world
And here I am
In my pyjamas

# 10 THOUSAND

It takes
10 Thousand hours
To be an expert
so let's try doing
10 Thousand hours
of Joy

# THE MONTHLY

Some days I lose hope
Nothing seems right in the world
I question everything
I cry my eyes out
The next day
I get my period
And it all makes sense again

# CONNECT THE DOTS

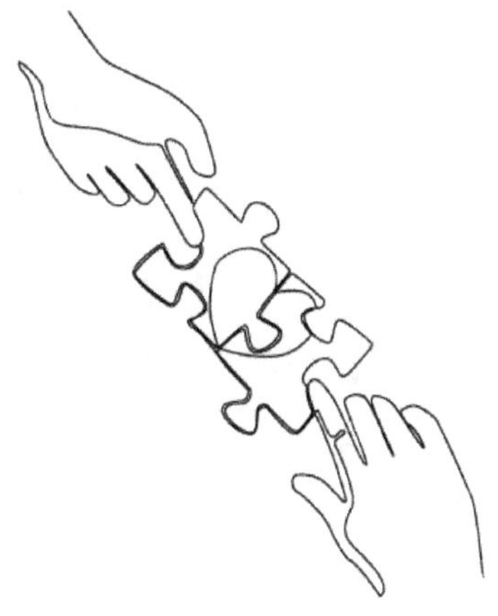

The length of a connection
Does not determine
The depth of a connection

# JOY

My goal
is to reach
The wanton abandon
and unbridled joy
of a child
Let my responsibilities rest for today

# SISTER

How have I been so lucky
to have found
Such bright lights
Such warm souls
Such wonderful people
that I get to call
My sisters

# HOW TO MAKE IT RIGHT

The days I'm low
all I have to do
Is call my sister

# IS IT MEANT TO BE?

Hope is a dangerous thing
When we hope for
Things not meant for us

# ALGEBRA

Whether in math
Or in life
Equations always
Need to balance

# RELATIONSHIP CYCLE

The way you made me feel
Like I could achieve anything
Like I had everything

The way you made me feel
Seen and heard and understood
Like we were two peas in a pod

The way you made me feel
Angry, frustrated and forlorn
Our love's era was bygone

The way you made me feel
With words unspoken
You left me heartbroken

Nevertheless, I wish you happiness
And hope you find someone
who makes you feel
The way you made me feel

# GRANDMOTHER

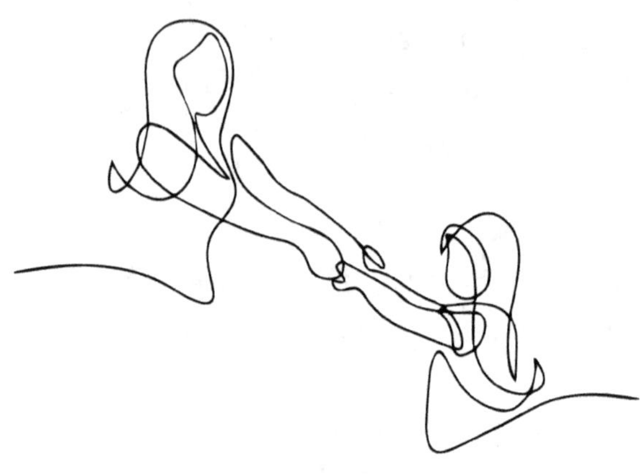

Mother of mothers
Maker of biryanis and treats
Keeper of family traditions
Fierce, resilient, loving
In the end
A grandmother is
A mother, only grander

# RE PLUG

Unlike our phones and laptops
We recharge when we unplug

# FILL THE CUP

It is such a beautiful thing
When
You put
Attention
Love
Energy
Effort
Into anything,
The ordinary becomes extraordinary

# LIKE A VIRGIN

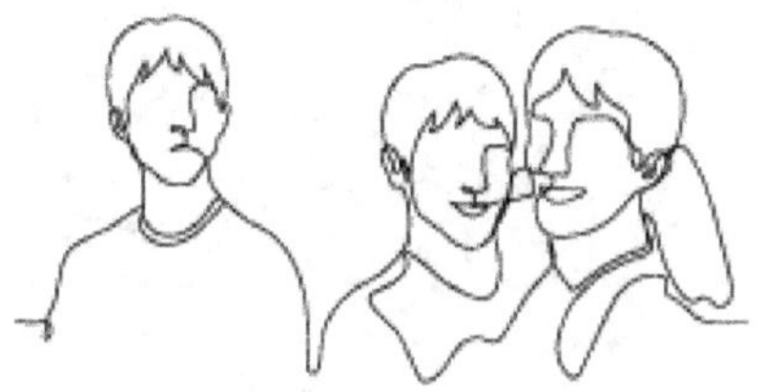

Everyone talks about
Losing their virginity
But what about
When you first lost
Your individuality
In an effort
To fit in?

# THE HIGHEST CURRENCY

So grateful
For all the love
I've been able to
Give and receive
My soul is immensely rich

# TREE OF LIFE

The roots, trunk and leaves
Are important too...
Then why
Do we only look at the flowers?

# SURVIVOR

Better times come
When we survive days
We thought we couldn't

# SOUL FOOD

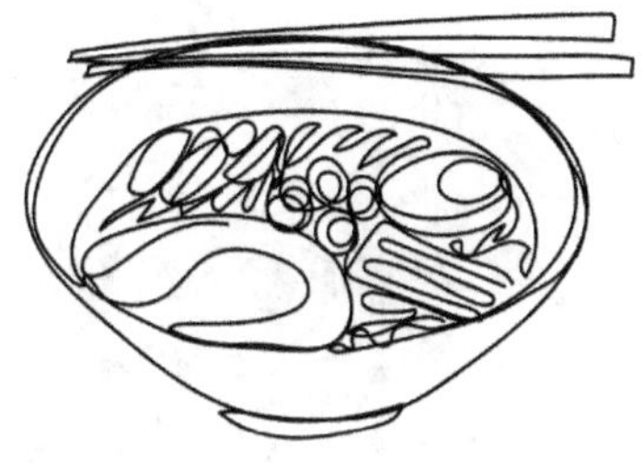

The language of love
World over
Is either sharing a meal
Or feeding someone
It is no question then
That I've loved
And been loved immensely

# CONTROL

All that we can control
In this whole wide world
Is ourselves

# FAIRYTALE

The frog to prince(ss) transformation
Took place
In reverse
When I kissed my baby;
From cool energetic girl
To uncool tired mom
Such is my fairytale

# CONSISTENCY

Seemingly mundane tasks
Done everyday
Could achieve all your goals...
If only I were a robot

# DIG DEEP

Going deeper into the pain
Gives us the root
Of where
To start
The healing

# WE CAN SEE THE CRACKS

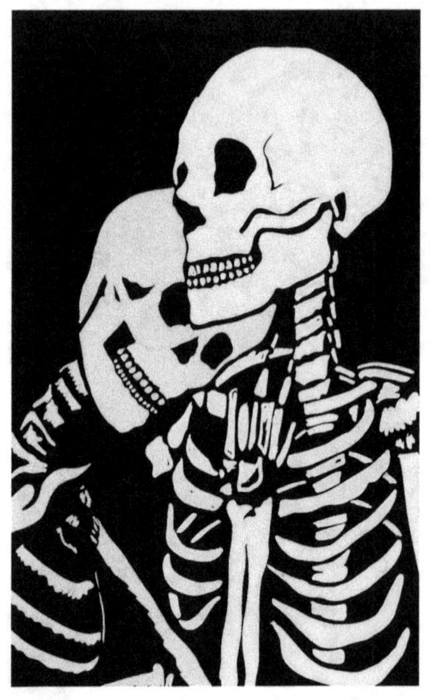

Bad times
Are like X-ray machines
For people's true characters

# EXISTENCE

Some days
I still can't believe
that we both exist in this world
but not with each other

# BE A MAN

Men's pain
Gets hidden
Driven deep down
In an effort to
"Be a man"

# IS A MILLION ENOUGH?

Your absence
Still hurts
Even after
I've bid you
A million goodbyes

# THE WAY

I love
The way
Your lips curve when you smile
The way
Your eyes take time to open up in the
morning
The way
Your hands move when you talk excitedly
The way seems brighter
With you

# ALL ABOUT ME

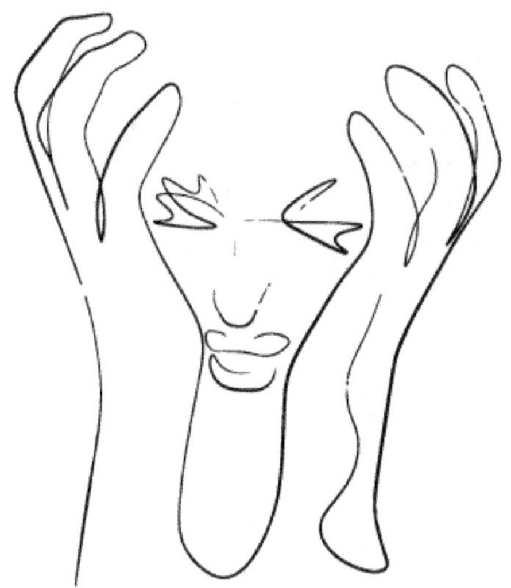

Who gave you permission
to walk all over yourself?
Who gave you permission
to put everyone else first?

# HOME

How did you know
My favourite smell
Was you?

# INSOMNIA

Sleep evades me
The nights
My thoughts invade me

# MY FRIEND

What is this sadness within me
Let me sit with it some time
Let me get to know it better
Let me hear what it has to say

# SUBMISSION

They said - you're no good
They said - why do this
They said - let it go
And I listened
And I suffered...

And I learnt better

# TIME TRAVEL

That one look
Exquisite
Piercing
Made me forget everything else
Makes me remember it always

# SPEECHLESS

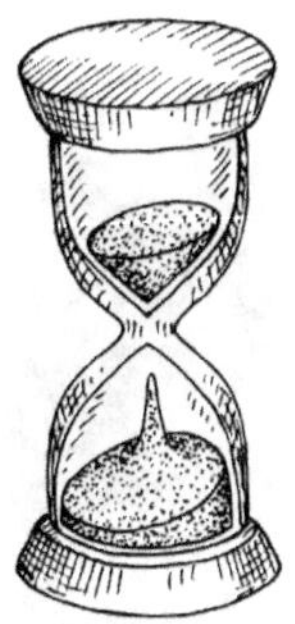

How can words describe
a moment a memory
a longing a languishing
a smile a secret

# GOODBYE

I have let you go,
Like they said I should
Yet
When I close my eyes and smile
You are the first thought in my mind

# MANIFESTATION

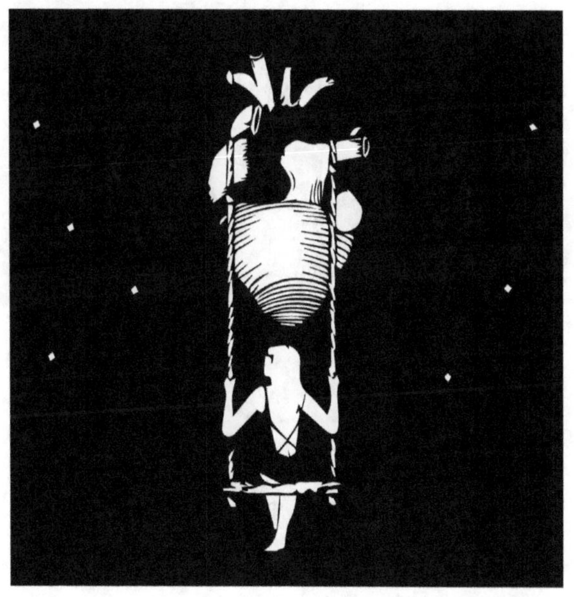

Speak the words
Believe
Feel
And so it is

# A PERFECT MOMENT IN TIME

My friend and I had just bought icecreams
She started laughing for no reason
it was infectious
in a moment
we were roaring with laughter together
crossing our legs
to prevent ourselves from peeing
Tears of joy streaming
The sea wind blowing in our faces;
A memory to last forever

# REAL QUESTIONS

Sometimes,
When I look back
At my younger days
My crushes and fashion choices,
My round Gandhiji-type glasses
My grand musical performances
How my friends were of utmost importance
The parents weren't cool they didn't know much
We knew everything better than them as such
School gossip and rumours
Teasing teachers was our humour
All of this and more makes me cringe
It makes me ask
The most important question...
What was I thinking?

# LIFE AFTER 40

It hurts
Where?
Everywhere.

# THE DANCE

There was a heavy boulder on my back
it made me look at the ground,
hunched in despair.
I tried to straighten up
but it was too heavy.
The only way was down,
falling to the ground,
and when I did
there was darkness.
I smelt the earth and lay there for some time
The only way from there was up
I had to be strong.
I turned my face to look at the sun
Slowly, the heavy burden slid off my back
and as I straightened my posture
I decided,
to stand up
and dance for a while.